Connell Short Guide

to

Strange Case of
Dr Jekyll and
Mr Hyde

*by David Anderson
and Jon Connell*

Contents

Introduction

Written in 1886, Robert Louis Stevenson's short novel was soon considered as a parable — or, as one literary critic has called it, a "fable". Indeed Stevenson's biographer Claire Harman argues that *Strange Case of Dr Jekyll and Mr Hyde* "is now so embedded in popular culture that it hardly exists as a work of literature". But *Jekyll and Hyde* is far more than just the tale of a "split personality". It's a masterpiece of narrative craft which, in England alone, sold 40,000 copies in the first six months after publication, and more than five times as many pirated copies in America.

The Characters

Dr Henry Jekyll
A respectable, wealthy doctor and scientist living in central London.

Mr Edward Hyde
The evil side of Jekyll – a villainous, violent rogue of squat stature, few words, and an indescribably terrifying expression. Occupies rented rooms in Soho, and given to obscure nocturnal wanderings through London.

Gabriel John Utterson
An upright and reserved lawyer, and "a lover of the sane and customary sides of life". He advises others compassionately, but his inclination to "Cain's heresy" suggests another side to his character: to suffer from Cain's heresy means to sympathise with the Biblical figure who denies responsibility for his wayward brother, Abel, and murders him.

Mr Guest
Utterson's head clerk, a reliable man and – crucially – "a great student and critic of handwriting".

Richard Enfield
A distant relative of Utterson, and a "well-known man about town": a louche, bohemian type, fond of using fashionable urban slang.

Dr Hastie Lanyon

A "hearty, healthy, dapper, red-faced gentleman, with a shock of hair prematurely white, and a boisterous and decided manner". Lives and works in Cavendish Square, Marylebone, a centre for the London medical profession. Once a close friend of Jekyll, but increasingly alienated by his "unscientific" investigations.

Mr Poole

Dr Jekyll's elderly servant. Has also been given orders to obey Mr Hyde.

Sir Danvers Carew

"An aged and beautiful gentleman with white hair" and a Member of Parliament, murdered by Hyde in cold blood.

Inspector Newcomen

Police officer tasked with solving Carew's murder.

Maidservant

Witness of Carew's murder.

A summary of the plot

1 "Story of the Door"

Strolling along a "by-street in a busy quarter of London", Gabriel Utterson and Richard Enfield come across an old, neglected doorway. It reminds Enfield of a strange story: walking home late one night, he saw an innocent young girl "trampled" just here by a vicious, angry man, moving like "some damned Juggernaut". Even more oddly, this man calmly offered to pay off his victim when Enfield collared him: from inside the doorway, he produced "ten pounds in gold and a cheque for the balance on Coutt's" — a nearby bank used by the wealthy.

Since the cheque was signed by a well-known, respectable man, Enfield and Utterson agree that there might be some kind of blackmail at the bottom of this strange affair. Out of politeness, Enfield doesn't mention who signed the cheque. And, frustratingly, the reader isn't told – even though Utterson seems to have guessed it. We do hear about the "Juggernaut": this man, named Hyde, had something "downright detestable" about him, but Enfield struggles to characterise it. Walking on, the two agree not to speak of the sad case again.

2 "Search for Mr Hyde"

Back at home, Utterson, a lawyer, looks up Dr Jekyll's will, which leaves all his possessions to his "friend and benefactor" Edward Hyde. It's now clear how he guessed the name on the cheque. He's more certain than ever about blackmail, fearing that the reason behind it is "disgrace" on Jekyll's part. Discussing the case with his friend Dr Lanyon, Utterson is surprised to discover that Lanyon and Jekyll haven't seen each other for over a decade, after Jekyll "began to go wrong, wrong in mind". And Lanyon has never heard of Hyde.

Utterson is plagued by dreams about the mysterious Hyde. He begins to "haunt" the doorway where the girl was trampled in the hope of meeting him. At last, Utterson gets an address — "a number of a street in Soho", which at the time was a poor and run-down neighbourhood. Dropping in on Jekyll, he finds that the doctor isn't in, but that his head servant Mr Poole has orders to obey Hyde. Now more certain than ever about blackmail, Utterson laments "the ghost of some old sin, the cancer of some concealed disgrace" that he imagines to be at the heart of this affair. He starts to fear that "if this Hyde suspects the existence of the will, he may grow impatient to inherit".

3 "Dr Jekyll was Quite At Ease"

Staying late after a dinner at Jekyll's house, Utterson inquires after the will. Jekyll, aggravated, doesn't want to speak of it, but assures Utterson that "the moment I choose, I can be rid of Mr Hyde". Jekyll has Utterson promise to see that his will is carried out should anything happen to him.

4 "The Carew Murder Case"

A year has passed. A maidservant sits in her window in a moonlit street, and sees an old man (the MP Sir Danvers Carew) encountering "a very small gentleman", who she recognises as Hyde. Hyde seems impatient, then suddenly snaps, battering the man with his heavy cane before trampling him "with an ape-like fury". At this point the maid faints.

Hyde's crime seems irrational: he hasn't stolen anything from Carew. The police find his purse and watch as well as a letter for Utterson, who recognises fragments of Hyde's cane from one he'd given to Jekyll years earlier, and offers to take Inspector Newcomen to Hyde's Soho address. He's not at home, but Hyde's rooms, in this "dismal quarter", are strangely furnished "with luxury and good taste". The other half of the stick is there, but there is disorder and evidence of papers having been burned. A visit to the bank shows "several thousand pounds" deposited in Hyde's name.

5 "Incident of the Letter"

At Jekyll's house, Utterson finds Jekyll "looking deadly sick" and insisting that he will have no more to do with Hyde. He shows Utterson a letter, signed by Hyde, declaring that he has escaped. Jekyll claims to have burned the envelope, and that the message was hand-delivered, yet his servant avers that nothing had arrived that day except by the main post.

Utterson later shows the letter to his head clerk Mr Guest, an expert in handwriting. Guest declares that it isn't the script of a madman: in fact, he recognises it as Dr Jekyll's. And when a note arrives that moment from Jekyll, the parallel is confirmed. "The two hands are in many points identical," says Guest, "only differently sloped". Utterson is horrified at the idea, thinking that his friend has forged the note to protect Hyde.

6 "Remarkable Incident of Dr Lanyon"

Time passes. Hyde is no longer seen, and Jekyll becomes more sociable. He, Utterson and Lanyon are as old friends again. Then, suddenly, Utterson is refused admittance to Jekyll's house. Six days later, he dines at Lanyon's, who seemed to have "grown pale; his flesh had fallen away; he was visibly balder and older". Lanyon says he has had a shock that he will not recover from, and that he regards Jekyll as dead, telling Utterson that "some day... after I am dead" he will find out the full story.

Within a fortnight Lanyon *is* dead, and a letter arrives with Utterson bearing the title "PRIVATE: for the hands of J.G. Utterson ALONE and in the case of his predecease *to be destroyed*". Inside, another sealed letter bares text claiming that it is "not to be opened till the death or disappearance of Dr Henry Jekyll". Frustrated, Utterson puts it in his safe. His visits to Jekyll become less frequent.

7 "Incident at the Window"

Utterson and Enfield are out walking again. When they happen to pass the door, Enfield remarks on Utterson not having mentioned that "this was a back way to Dr Jekyll's". Approaching, they see the doctor at a window. Jekyll turns down a stroll with the two cousins, but seems pleased to chat for a while, before all at once "the smile was struck out of his face and succeeded by an expression of such abject terror and despair, as froze the blood of the two gentlemen below". The window closes suddenly, and the walkers turn pale and continue in silence.

8 "The Last Night"

Mr Poole arrives at Utterson's house in a cold sweat.

Returning to Jekyll's, the two are admitted by servants "huddled together like a flock of sheep" in the hall. Poole leads Utterson through the house and loudly announces the lawyer's presence. The dismissive answer, issuing from a locked room, doesn't sound like Jekyll.

Whoever is in the room has been casting notes on to the stairwell, repeatedly demanding things from the local chemist and complaining about what they supply. The handwriting, observes Utterson, is "unquestionably" Jekyll's, but Poole insists that he has seen the occupant of the room, and that he clearly resembles Hyde.

The two arm themselves and prepare to enter: five axe-blows fell the heavy door, revealing a strangely serene scene of "quiet lamplight" and orderly papers, "a good fire chattering on the hearth, the kettle singing its thin strain... the things laid out for tea". The body of Hyde, dressed in clothes "far too large for him, clothes of the doctor's bigness" lies lifeless on the floor.

Unsurprisingly – to us, at least – there's no sign of Jekyll's body, but there is a will leaving Jekyll's possessions to Utterson. It doesn't make sense that Hyde would have left this intact, and Utterson's "head goes round" in confusion. With the will is a note written that day, telling Utterson to read "the narrative which Lanyon warned me he was to place in your hands; and if you care to hear more, turn to the confession of, Your unworthy and unhappy friend, HENRY JEKYLL".

9 "Dr Lanyon's Narrative"

This chapter is a transcript of Lanyon's letter. It describes how he came to witness Hyde's transformation into Jekyll, and how his friend offered him a choice: "Will you be wise?" he asked, "will you be guided? will you suffer me to take this glass in my hand and to go forth from your house without further parley? or has the greed of curiosity too much to command of you?"

Hyde's language mockingly parodies that of Lanyon's own moralistic criticisms of Jekyll, but Lanyon tells how he submitted, and witnessed the transformation scene: Hyde "reeled, staggered, clutched at the table and held on, staring with injected eyes, gasping with an open mouth" before Jekyll stood there "like a man restored from death". This is the first time that we, as readers, witness the transformation, even if we already guessed that Jekyll and Hyde are one and the same person.

10 "Henry Jekyll's Full Statement of the Case"

This last chapter is Jekyll's "confession", which takes the form of a history of his own life. He begins by describing the sense of split personality that had bothered him since childhood, and his early experiments to separate the "two natures". Then he tells of the experience of transformation itself — "a grinding in the bones, deadly nausea, and a horror of the spirit" followed by a sense of being "younger, lighter, happier in body" and "conscious of a heady recklessness".

Jekyll claims that his drug "had no discriminating action". He means that he could have become good or evil, depending on his state of mind. The problem was, he inevitably turned to it at moments when his "virtue slumbered", doing awful deeds and being forced into attempting to "undo" their consequences afterwards. Later, he recounts having woken up one morning as Hyde without having taken the potion — an experience that frightened him enough to reject Hyde for a while. Yet the next time he took the draft, Hyde re-asserted himself with a vengeance, and it was on this occasion that he murdered Sir Carew.

After that, Jekyll resolved on a "beneficent and innocent life". But this was just another extreme in the increasingly acute fluctuations of his character. He describes how, one day in Spring, a simple proud thought led to his suddenly changing into Hyde — again, without the aid of the drug. Managing to get home (despite Hyde now being a wanted man) he planned the demonstration to Lanyon, but he kept slipping into Hyde's form.

"From that day forth," reads his confession, "it seemed only by a great effort as of gymnastics, and only under the immediate stimulation of the drug, that I was able to wear the countenance of Jekyll."

This document — the text which we are reading — was written "under the influence of the last of the old powders": unable to acquire the necessary ingredients from the chemist, Jekyll has resigned himself to remaining Hyde forever, starting "half an hour from now". He wonders with horror what will happen next — but we already know, because it did happen, two chapters ago.

What is *Jekyll and Hyde* about?

Should we take Robert Louis Stevenson seriously as a writer for grown-ups? The question was posed back in 1950, a hundred years after Stevenson's death, by one of America's most brilliant and provocative critics, Leslie Fiedler.

No one, of course, said Fiedler, disputed that the author of *Treasure Island* was good at telling stories for children. But adults? There had always been, and remained, doubts about his status as a "serious" novelist. Take *Jekyll and Hyde**. We can acknowledge it's a tragedy, said Fiedler, "but its allegory is too schematic, too slightly realised in terms of fiction

*   The full title under which Stevenson published the novel is *The Strange Case of Dr Jekyll and Mr Hyde*. For simplicity's sake, we refer to the story throughout by its widely used shorter version – *Jekyll and Hyde*

and character... while its explicit morality demands that evil be portrayed finally as an obvious monster".

C. Keith, writing in the same year as Fiedler, was equally damning. Yes *Jekyll and Hyde* has a moral, he said:

> Oh, but a blatant one! If you weren't careful, the evil in you would swallow up the good, as the wicked Hyde does to Dr Jekyll. And you'd be lost. So be careful!

These dismissive views of Stevenson's art, however, were not typical at the time, and few critics nowadays would agree with them. This is partly because there has been a thorough reappraisal since the 1950s not just of Stevenson, but of the whole tradition of Gothic literature to which *Jekyll and Hyde* belongs. It is also because many modern critics – especially Freudian and Marxist critics – hugely admire his dissection of Victorian society.

It has been argued, for example, that in popular fiction it is the *images* – the vivid portrayals of people and events – which matter most, while in serious fiction, as in novels by the likes of George Eliot and Henry James, *analysis* trumps images.

On the face of it, much of the analysis in *Jekyll and Hyde* is strikingly crude. But as William Veeder and Gordon Hirsch have argued, the "self-analytic ineptitudes" in the novel derive not from the author but from the characters. "*Jekyll and Hyde* engages ineptly in self-analysis in order to call into question the very possibility of such analysis". In other words the novel is dealing with material which is very difficult, even impossible, to analyse.

Critics who argue otherwise, one might add, are making the same mistake as those who criticise Conrad for being long-winded in *Heart of Darkness*. In truth the fault of long-windedness really lies not with Conrad but with his narrator, Marlow. It is deliberate because Marlow can't bear to face the truth so shields himself from it with a fog of words.

Stevenson's short novel, often referred to as a novella, is an immensely complex piece of work, open to all kinds of interpretations. It is also strikingly modern. "Is *Dr Jekyll and Mr Hyde* a work of philosophic intention, or simply the most ingenious and irresponsible of fictions?" asked Henry James, a friend of Stevenson's. His answer was very much the former.

Stevenson, says the crime writer Ian Rankin, wanted to explore the various facets of human nature. "Was civilisation just a thin veneer?" What happened if you scratched away its surface "to reveal the truth beneath"? *Jekyll and Hyde* is an important story, says Rankin, because it discusses the problem of how human beings can do terrible things to one another. "Jekyll feels hidebound in his own skin, made to comply with the rigid conventions of his class and society, Hyde frees him from this,

*   *Dr Jekyll and Mr Hyde after One Hundred Years,* edited by William Veeder and Gordon Hirsch

Richard Mansfield was best known for the dual role depicted in this double exposure: he starred in Dr. Jekyll and Mr. Hyde *in both New York and London*

but the sensation of liberation is addictive." It is no accident that Hyde is described as being much younger than Jekyll, a man past 50 who regrets the opportunities he has missed. "The folly of youth – the sense of possibility and invincibility – is regained when he becomes Edward Hyde."

It is worth noting, incidentally, the debt that Stevenson owed to Mary Shelley, the author of *Frankenstein. Frankenstein,* like *Jekyll and Hyde,* falls under the umbrella of Gothic fiction which, as Peter Garrett has put it, has a "characteristic complication of narrative form and multiplication of voices" so as to deepen the mystery. The narrative

*   From *Dr Jekyll & Mr Hyde after One Hundred Years*

device in *Jekyll and Hyde*, as in *Frankenstein*, reflects the story's theme of a force that cannot be controlled. The difference is that in *Frankenstein* the force is a monster, created by a human being but existing in its own right as a separate creature.

So Stevenson, in effect, *inverts* the story of *Frankenstein*, "by gradually revealing the monstrous nature of a human creator rather than the human nature of a monstrous creation".[*] He achieves this, like Shelley, by using multiple narratives which gradually reveal the monstrous perpetrators of a crime through the perpetrator's eventual confession. Both novels suggest that there is a monstrous side to human beings – and both suggest that some event can easily trigger it.

What makes the story so modern?

In 1886, the year *Jekyll and Hyde* first appeared, the great German philosopher Friedrich Nietzsche published a treatise called *Beyond Good and Evil*. The fundamental belief of most philosophers, wrote Nietzsche, is the "faith in opposite values". But these philosophers were wrong: humans are more

*   Ben Fuller "The Anxiety of the Unforeseen in Stevenson's *Jekyll and Hyde*".

complex than that. You can't simply divide them, or their natures, into categories as bald as good and evil.

The same thought underlies *Jekyll and Hyde*. To describe it as the story of a "split personality" is to over-simplify what Stevenson is saying. Look at the concluding section – Jekyll's "Full Statement". Even as he, Jekyll, talks about "the thorough and primitive duality of man", confirming the traditional notion that "man is... truly two", he immediately undercuts this by admitting that he might be wrong.

I say two, because the state of my knowledge does not pass beyond that point. Others will follow, others will outstrip me on the same lines; and I hazard the guess that man will ultimately be known for a mere polity of multifarious, incongruous and independent denizens.

Human beings are divided; we are all multiple personalities. What *Jekyll and Hyde* shows us, in Peter Garrett's words, is a "disunified model of the self" replacing the "traditional dualities".

The shifting relations between Jekyll and Hyde is evident in the grammar. As the narrator of his final "Statement" Jekyll is "I" but as the protagonist he is sometimes "I", sometimes "he" or "Jekyll", while Hyde is sometimes replaced by "I".

The pleasures which I made haste to seek in my disguise were, as I have said, undignified... The familiar that I called out of my own soul, and sent forth alone to do his good pleasure, was a being inherently malign and villainous; his every act and thought centred on self... Henry Jekyll stood at times aghast before the acts of Edward Hyde...

Great 19th century novels like *Great Expectations* and *Jane Eyre* charted the life of a character from adolescence to adulthood, and the simultaneous development of self-knowledge and judgement. *Jekyll and Hyde* does almost the opposite. Its unsatisfactory conclusion suggests the disintegration of personality rather than the acquiring of self-knowledge. The sense of alienation Jekyll feels, and the way Stevenson deals with it, brings the novel closer in tone and effect to the plays of the modern post-war playwright Samuel Beckett – and the aptly named Theatre of the Absurd – than to the traditional 19th century novel.

Jekyll and Hyde, says Ronald Thomas, launches "an elaborate assault on the ideals of the individual personality and the cult of character that dominated the 19th century".[*] Instead of watching a character become gradually integrated into a community, we witness instead Jekyll's "sudden disintegration".

We see, in other words, not progress but regression. Jekyll's story begins with "preparations

*   From *Dr Jekyll and Mr Hyde after One Hundred Years*

for its end". The first thing we know about him is that he has written a will. What we see is a professional man with a good reputation become a recluse, a murderer, and in the end a suicide.

And this breakdown is more than a moral, social and psychological one; it is a philosophical one as well. Not only does the main character disintegrate over the course of the text, but the whole notion of character is undermined.

Jekyll himself notes that he has become an "incongruous compound" of "dissociated" and "independent... elements". "Think of it," he says. "I did not even exist!" And by the end he doesn't exist. He has lost his will and his identity. By the end of the text he can only speak of another, not himself. "He, I say – I cannot say I". And before anyone reads the narrative he has written, as Thomas says, he has "literally and permanently disappeared".

The breakdown of personality corresponds, as Thomas also says, to a breakdown in "narrative conventions". Instead of coherent chapters we have ten disparate documents described as letters, incidents, cases and statements. The plot itself is barely coherent. In the first document or section, "The Story of the Door", the story being told is even called a "bad story" by its teller, Enfield, because it is "far from explaining" the mystery it dwells on. To quote Thomas again, the world we have been plunged into is one of "vain searches, unexplained disappearances, random incidents, and incomplete statements".

At the turn of the century, in the years after *Jekyll and Hyde*, the notion that the self was incoherent became steadily more prominent: a general unease about the nature of the self is central to the works of Nietzsche, and of Freud, and to the novels of, among others, Joseph Conrad, whose *Heart of Darkness* was published 14 years later in 1900.

In what sense is the novel a detective story?

"Please completely forget, disremember, obliterate, unlearn, consign to oblivion any notion you may have had that *Jekyll and Hyde* is some kind of mystery story, a detective story, or movie," Vladimir Nabokov told his students at Cornell University. Nabokov was being typically provocative. He saw all these genres as examples of "low" culture. In the same lecture he said comparing the cinema to the theatre is like comparing an undertaker to a mortician.

So Nabokov's advice shouldn't be taken literally. The context of mystery and detective fiction is in fact crucial to the novel, as its full title, *Strange Case of Jekyll and Hyde*, suggests.

We should bear in mind, too, that it was only a year after Stevenson's work first appeared that

The stuff of nightmares: Robert Louis Stevenson (1850 - 1894)

fiction's greatest detective, Sherlock Holmes, made his first appearance. Sir Arthur Conan Doyle, the man who made detective fiction popular, published *A Study in Scarlet* in 1887.

John Cawelti, in his study of detective fiction, shows how the genre descended directly from gothic fiction – from the dark mysteries of writers like Edgar Allan Poe. There are three elements in the formula for a classic detective story, thought Cawelti: a mystery, with certain facts concealed; an inquiry into the mystery, with the aid of an "inquirer-protagonist"; and an ending in which the concealed facts are made known.

*   John G. Cawelti, *Adventure, Mystery and Romance: Formula Stories as Art and Popular Culture* (1976)

There is certainly a mystery in *Jekyll and Hyde*, indeed there are many: what is Hyde's hold over Jekyll? Why is there an unprovoked attack on Sir Danvers Carew? How does Hyde then disappear so completely? Why does Jekyll go into isolation and why does he slam his window shut and retreat to his cabinet "with an expression of abject terror and despair"?

There is also an "inquirer-protagonist": Utterson. As Gordon Hirsch points out, Utterson does at first display "some of the acumen of the detective-hero". [*] In the first chapter, he seizes on Enfield's story with a confidence in his powers of observation, declaring that he doesn't need to be told the signature on Hyde's cheque "because I know it already".

Soon afterwards, he begins the search for Hyde with the much quoted line: "If he be Mr Hyde... I shall be Mr Seek." Like many a more conventional detective, he thinks the odd things he has seen have a simple explanation.

> *If he could but once set eyes on [Hyde], he thought the mystery would lighten, and perhaps roll altogether away, as was the habit of mysterious things when well examined.*

He doesn't make much progress, however, though he makes plenty of guesses in his quest for a rational

* From an essay in *Dr Jekyll and Mr Hyde after One Hundred Years*

explanation of what is happening. So when Poole comes to him to suggest Hyde has murdered Jekyll and is now in Jekyll's laboratory, Utterson dismisses the idea.

What could induce the murderer to stay? That won't hold water; it doesn't commend itself to reason. He even tries to explain away the strange figure he sees, who seems to be wearing a "mask upon his face". Just before they break down the door of Jekyll's locked apartment, Utterson says:

> These are very strange circumstances... but I think I begin to see daylight. Your master, Poole, is plainly seized with one of those maladies that both torture and deform the sufferer; hence the mask and avoidance of friends...

As usual he's wrong, and his inability to find a consistent rational explanation for events shows that while *Jekyll and Hyde* may seem in some respects like a detective story it isn't one. Indeed Stevenson rejects the whole framework of rationalist assumptions on which the detective genre rests.

Utterson is far from a typical, level-headed detective. Although he is "a lover of the sane and customary sides of life, to whom the fanciful was immodest", he is from the start of his search immersed in a nightmarish world. He feels, he says, "a nausea and distaste of life". In fact, he shares more than he knows with Jekyll/Hyde; he, too, is a

FIVE FACTS ABOUT
JEKYLL AND HYDE

---

1. Jekyll and Hyde has been adapted for the screen at least 44 times. The oldest surviving adaptation dates from 1912. Like many subsequent versions, it flies in the face of Stevenson's original by beginning with the transformation scene. The novel has also proved a hit with musicians: perhaps the most charismatic rendering was recorded in 1968 as a duet between the French singer Serge Gainsbourg and the actress Brigitte Bardot.

2. John Hunter, whose house in Leicester Square might have been the model for Dr. Jekyll's, was an avid collector of zoological specimens, including exotic animals and even the remains of deformed and diseased people, which he used for the education of trainee surgeons. His collection, which once ran to almost 14,000 objects, is now kept at the Royal College of Surgeons at Lincoln's Inn Fields, London.

3. In the sense that he "experiments" on himself, Dr Jekyll's activities were not unprecedented. One of his most famous forerunners was Sir Isaac Newton, whose investigations into vision in the 1660s involved poking a sharp instrument behind his own eyeball, in the hope that he could induce the sensation of seeing colours. Newton's notebooks contain a diagram of the grisly experiment.

4. In the essay "A Chapter on Dreams", Stevenson remarks that he wrote an earlier version of Jekyll and Hyde under the title The Travelling Companion, which "was returned by an editor on the plea that it was a work of genius and indecent, and which I burned the other day on the ground that it was not a work of genius, and that Jekyll had supplanted it".

5. When the first stage adaptation of the novel opened at the Lyceum theatre in London in 1888 (where Bram Stoker, author of Dracula, was the manager), the "transformation" of its leading actor Richard Mansfield was thought to be so convincing that he almost became a suspect in 1889's notorious "Jack the Ripper" murders. In fact, the situation grew so tense that the play was suspended in October, after the Ripper's first four murders.

divided personality who fantasises about "the lives of down-going men". He is "an inquiring detective", says Gordon Hirsch, "who really does not want to know, a Mr Seek who does not in fact want to find".

Behind what is superficially a detective story, then, Stevenson is making a broader point which undermines the whole notion of detective stories. Society, he suggests, places its faith in reason, yet the way society is organised is not reasonable. Instead of encouraging openness it encourages suppression. The rational and scientific, says Hirsch, are identified "with the respectable and with the self-satisfaction that accompanies respectability".

Anything which seems irrational, in other words, is not respectable. Utterson and Lanyon, we are told, are "thorough respectors of themselves and each other". Sir Danvers Carew has a look of "well-founded self-content". Appropriately, Jekyll's most terrifying transformation into Hyde happens on the park bench in a moment of "vainglorious thought" when Sir Danvers feels "safe of all men's respect, wealthy, beloved". Carew and the professional figures in the novel equate being respectable with the kind of rationality characteristic of a typical detective novel.

Yet Stevenson thinks there is no such thing as disinterested rationalism, no matter how much his characters may insist on it. They live in a world where, if something seemingly irrational disturbs their self-content, it has to be suppressed. Utterson hopes, for the sake of his friend Jekyll, that Hyde will not be brought to trial. *Jekyll and Hyde*, therefore, undercuts the detective novel at every turn. Hirsch writes:

> *Utterson cannot reasonably deduce anything, and his logic consistently fails him in a nearly laughable way because the mystery he seeks to solve is at its core a supernatural one, a gothic one – namely, that Jekyll has divided himself by means of a chemical potion, that Hyde is Jekyll, transmogrified.*

In most detective stories, the gothic doesn't feature. What might appear to be supernatural or inexplicable, as in the case of Conan Doyle's *Hound of the Baskervilles*, just isn't. The mysteriously glowing hound, in Conan Doyle's story, turns out just to be an ordinary wild dog treated with phosphorescent paint. *Jekyll and Hyde*, on the other hand, has a mystery which can't be solved in the way Holmes solves the mystery of the hound. We are in gothic territory, says Hirsch.

> The novel's terror... comes from losing control over the parts of the self, from losing any sense of a coherent personal identity... There is a sense, in other words, of the corrosive presence of gothic passion in a narrative that might look to be organised as detective fiction.

In effect, Stevenson's novel is a satire on the

traditional detective novel and a savage critique of the smug, repressive rationalism thought by its denizens to underly patriarchal society. For Sherlock Holmes, reason reigns supreme. For Stevenson, it doesn't.

What's striking about *Jekyll and Hyde*, says Ronald Thomas, is that it ends as a detective story usually begins – with the discovery of a corpse and/ or the unexplained disappearance of a character.* Instead of a story which moves towards a resolution we have a fragmentary, contradictory and incomplete narrative. "The incoherency of life," says Jekyll, "which was daily growing more unwelcome" also finally overwhelms the story itself. Thomas writes:

> In the confusion into which Jekyll's wild and strange life story dissolves, things don't continue or conclude. They don't weave themselves into a conclusion. They just stop.

One way of reading *Jekyll and Hyde* is to see it as an exploration of the criminal mind: "its interests are much more deeply rooted in the divided personality of the criminal who eventually becomes his own victim". Here the "criminal intellect" is not some separate entity. Instead criminals are on the surface respected and upright citizens.

In his final statement, Jekyll describes his

---

* Ronald R. Thomas, *Dreams of Authority* (1990)

schizophrenic existence:

> *A moment before I had been safe of all men's respect, wealthy, beloved – the cloth laying for me in the dining-room at home; and now I was the common quarry of mankind, hunted, houseless, a known murderer, thrall to the gallows.*

Is *Jekyll and Hyde* about repression?

Why, apart from a fleeting appearance by the maidservant who faints when she witnesses Carew's murder, are there no women in *Jekyll and Hyde*? And why are the major characters, Jekyll, Utterson and Lanyon, "all professional men as well as celibates"?

Posing these questions, the critic William Veeder says they lead us to one of the central concerns of Stevenson's novel, namely "the inherent weakness of late-Victorian social organisation".

The story is nominally set in London, but its real setting is the "larger milieu of the late-Victorian patriarchy". In his treatment of it, Stevenson reflects what is often thought to be the "autumnal" quality of late-Victorian life – the sense that

* From an essay in *Dr Jekyll and Mr Hyde after One Hundred Years*, edited by William Veeder and Gordon Hirsch

patriarchy is past its peak, that an era is coming to an end, that something is the matter with society which needs to be rectified.

Jekyll and Hyde reflects strongly this sense of anxiety about the loss of authority, an authority which in Victorian England was emphatically male. Stevenson himself seems to have been conflicted about Britain and in particular the British empire, his sense of pride in imperial achievements increasingly tinged by a sense of guilt.

To put it at its simplest, *Jekyll and Hyde,* says Veeder, is "an indictment of Victorian repressiveness, a tale of decorum and desire". Many critics agree on this, but what exactly is it that is being repressed? Pleasure? Homosexuality? Sexuality in general? Love?

Different critics give different answers. It is not pleasure, says Veeder. The men in *Jekyll and Hyde* are not joyless. Utterson and co are capable of genuine friendship: the word "friend" appears at least 33 times in the story. There are "pleasant dinners" hosted by Jekyll, who entertains "five or six old cronies" early in the story. Jekyll's entrance hall is called "the pleasantest room in London".

Stevenson could have ridiculed his group of men, as he did other bourgeois males who

> had at first a human air
> In coats and flannel underwear.
> They rose and walked upon their feet
> And filled their bellies full of meat.

They wiped their lips when they had done,
But they were Ogres every one.*

The men in *Jekyll and Hyde* are by no means "Ogres every one". Stevenson wishes, in his life and in *Jekyll and Hyde*, that men were "less hypocritical about pleasures natural and healthy, and even pleasures unnatural and unhealthy", says Veeder, but the novelist's point is not that his characters are incapable of enjoying themselves. It is that their pleasures would be greater, and they would be happier, if they weren't so repressed.

So what makes them repressed? Veeder cites the great psychologist Sigmund Freud. Freud argued that we have no control over our unconscious — a troubling thought, but one which clearly fits Jekyll's relationship to Hyde. Jekyll even describes identity as a "fortress", specifically anticipating Freud's idea that the conscious mind acts to limit the effects of primal urges hidden beneath the surface.

The fact that the novel was inspired by a dream – Freud described dreams as the "royal road to a knowledge of the unconscious activities of the mind" – is predictably seized on by critics. Mr Hyde first appeared to Stevenson as a grotesque and mysterious figure in a dream, his biographer, Jenni Calder, tells us – and this is also how Hyde first appears to Utterson, in a troubling dream about his friend Dr Jekyll.

* Jenni Calder, *Robert Louis Stevenson: A Life Study* (1980)

Freud's most controversial theory was that all men pass through a phase in which they wish to murder their fathers and have sexual intercourse with their mothers. The theory, now a familiar one, is known as the Oedipus complex – and Freud's most famous example of the Oedipus complex in action was Hamlet in Shakespeare's play. Hamlet's behaviour, said Freud, could be explained if we understand that what he subconsciously wanted to do was murder his father and make love to his mother.

So how does Freud's theory explain *Jekyll and Hyde*? Stevenson, argues William Veeder, had a troubled relationship with his father, with whom he constantly argued. Indeed, shortly after his father died, he exclaimed: "I almost begin to feel I should care to live; I would, by God! And so I begin to feel I shall." In *Jekyll and Hyde*, says Veeder – pointing out that the very name Jekyll hides the homicidal phrase "je kyll" – it is no accident that the man brutally murdered by Hyde, Sir Danvers Carew, is "a beautiful gentleman with white hair", who, Veeder argues, "can stand in for the [then] aging but still strikingly handsome Thomas Stevenson". Robert Louis Stevenson can then deploy "literary patricide" to murder a substitute father figure.

Does this Freudian view have any credibility? We should remember that there is no evidence in support of the Oedipus complex – it is a theory, and one, moreover, that is impossible either to prove or to disprove. There is no doubt, however, that Stevenson shared Freud's fascination about the unconscious, and that *Jekyll and Hyde* is concerned above all else with repression.

How important is homo-sexuality in the novel?

So we return to the question: what exactly is it that is being repressed in *Jekyll and Hyde*?

In 1886, the year the novel was written, the idea of people having multiple personalities was quickly gaining ground. It wasn't only Nietzsche who was pondering it. So were English pyschologists in The Journal of Mental Science: they were fascinated by a case in France involving an adolescent street urchin known as Louis V, who had once been happy and well-behaved but then suddenly became violent, greedy and quarrelsome. What was odder was that he then seemed to embrace and revel in his new personality. It was a case of what came at the time to be known as "male hysteria".

Stevenson is likely to have read about this case. As he will also have been aware, homosexuality was a subject of great scientific interest in 1886. By the 1880s, as later scholars have shown, the Victorian homosexual world had become a secret though highly active subculture. And for most middle-class inhabitants of this world, as the American critic

Elaine Showalter says, homosexuality "represented a double life".[*]

Stevenson, argues Showalter, was "the fin-de-siecle laureate of the double life". He always felt, as he confessed, a "strong sense of man's double being". Even as a student in Edinburgh he had dreamt of leading "a double life – one of the day, one of the night". So far as we know Stevenson had no homosexual leanings, though he undoubtedly possessed the power to make other men fall in love with him. Among his circle, says Jenni Calder, "male appreciation of Stevenson was often intensely physical".[**]

But the issue in *Jekyll and Hyde* is not Stevenson's own sexuality. It is "his sense of the fantasies beneath the surface of daylight decorum", as Showalter puts it:

> ...the shadow of homosexuality that surrounded Clubland and the nearly hysterical terror of revealing forbidden emotions between men that constituted the dark side of the patriarchy.

Jekyll and Hyde can thus "most persuasively be read as a fable of fin-de-siecle homosexual panic, the discovery and resistance of the homosexual self".

Not only is this a very male story, it is a story about middle-aged bachelors whose only

[*] Elaine Sbowalter, *Sexual Anarchy: Gender and Culture at the Fin de Siècle* (1991)
[**] Jenni Calder, *Robert Louis Stevenson*

relationships with women are with servants. And they're all celibates – Mr Stevenson, wrote Alice Brown in 1895, "is a boy who has no mind to play with girls". The tale, as it develops, said the critic Stephen Gwynn, "might almost be one of a community of monks".

Unable to pair off with either a woman or another man, argues Showalter, Jekyll divides himself and finds "his only mate" in his double, Hyde. Jekyll never actually admits what his sexual desires are, but he admits to feeling "a profound duplicity of life" and "an almost morbid sense of shame". He longs to separate his mind and his body. "If each, I told myself, could be housed in separate identities, life would be relieved of all that was unbearable."

Utterson, the lawyer who is the central narrator is "scanty and embarrassed in discourse" and "undemonstrative". But, like Jekyll, as we've seen, he has an unconventional side: he identifies with the high spirits of "down-going men". "I incline to Cain's fantasy," he says. "I let my brother go to the devil in his own way." And perhaps because he is so repressed he becomes "enslaved" (his word) by the mystery of Hyde.

Images of forced penetration through locked doors into cabinets, rooms and closets permeate Utterson's narrative. Indeed, says Showalter, "the organising image for this narrative is the breaking down of doors, learning the secret behind them". In the last chapter, Utterson even breaks down the door to Jekyll's private closet with an axe, as if into what Jekyll calls "the very fortress of identity".

Not surprisingly, Jekyll's bachelor friends worry about what Utterson thinks of as his "strange preference" for Edward Hyde. Why has he willed away his estate to what they see as a loutish young man? Even when Hyde is suspected of a crime, Jekyll tries to shield him. "I do sincerely take a great, a very great interest in that young man," he tells Utterson.

Jekyll's obsession with Hyde can be seen as reflecting a tendency among the upper middle classes in Victorian times to idealise young working class men. The crossing of class barriers, the search for what was called "rough trade", preoccupied a number of prominent homosexuals, among them the novelist E.M. Forster, who admitted to fantasising about "a strong young man of the working class".

In his original draft of the manuscript, Stevenson was more explicit about the sexual leanings which drove Jekyll to a double life. Jekyll had become, we're told in that draft, "from an early age... a slave of certain appetites" which were "at once criminal in the sight of the law and abhorrent in themselves. They cut me off from the sympathy of those whom I otherwise respected."

In the final draft these passages were cut but the sense of abnormality which surrounds Hyde is retained. The male characters uniformly feel "disgust, loathing and fear" when they think of him.

There is plenty of imagery in the novel, as we've

noted, which can be seen as reinforcing the idea of homosexuality, and of its being a criminal offence. An obvious example is Jekyll's house, with its two entrances. Hyde always enters it through the back door which, in Stevenson's words, is "equipped with neither bell nor knocker". And the suicide which ends Jekyll's narrative is the only appropriate ending. As A.E. Housman would write in *A Shropshire Lad*:

> Shot? so quick, so clean an ending?
> Oh that was right, lad, that was brave:
> Yours was not an ill for mending,
> 'Twas best to take it to the grave.

What was Stevenson's own view of *Jekyll and Hyde*?

Plenty of commentators have pointed to the homosexual undertones of *Jekyll and Hyde*. Vladimir Nabokov suggested that the "all-male pattern" of the novel evoked notions of "homosexual practices so common in London behind the Victorian veil", whether Stevenson intended it or not. Elaine Showalter thinks Stevenson was writing about the repressions caused by society's taboo against homosexuals.

So what about Stevenson himself? What did he

say about the story after writing it? It's at least worth considering this when we judge it, even if novelists aren't always the best judges of their own novels. Take the letter Stevenson wrote to his friend John Bocock, an American journalist, a year or so after *Jekyll and Hyde* was published. He was reacting to Bocock's account of a sensational stage portrayal of Hyde in New York which showed Hyde as a sexual predator, threatening his "fiancée", a new character specially invented for the stage version.

In reply, Stevenson wrote an exasperated letter about the Victorian tendency to link sexual appetite to evil. The problem, said Stevenson, was not Hyde's sexual appetite. It was Jekyll's attempt to conceal his nature.

> Hyde was... not, Great Gods! a mere voluptuary [someone devoted to sensual pleasure]. There is no harm in a voluptuary; and none, with my hand on my heart and in the sight of God, none – no harm whatsoever – in what prurient fools call "immorality". The harm was in Jekyll, because he was a hypocrite – not because he was fond of women... The Hypocrite let out the beast Hyde – who is no more sexual than another, but who is the essence of cruelty and malice, and selfishness and cowardice: and these are the diabolic in man – not this poor wish to have a woman, that they make such a cry about.

As Katherine Linehan points out, Stevenson had

also dwelt on this theme in an essay written seven years before he wrote the novel. In this, too, he makes the point that sexual desire is not harmful; it can be a vehicle for either good or ill for the human soul, depending on whether it serves as a force for self-integration or self-alienation. We are mentally healthiest, and live most fully, Stevenson said, when are sensual faculties or desires align with our "conscience" or "inner self or soul". The glory of wholehearted love, he suggested, can bring the senses into harmony with the best impulses of mind and conscience.

On the other hand when body and soul are divided by the demands of sexuality then it causes a severe form of estrangement. Jekyll is a hypocrite; he is divided; that is the cause of his misery.

Stevenson's talk about the soul is a reminder that he was brought up as a Scottish Presbyterian in Edinburgh. He had been taught to believe, like all Presbyterians, that small sins can become large ones if we try to hide them and don't listen to what our conscience tells us. It was a belief he always retained, coupled with his belief in the power of love.

Stevenson's ideas about love are played out in reverse in *Jekyll and Hyde*, says Katherine Linehan, in particular, as she puts it, his belief in "love's capacity to promote psychic self-unification and

* Katherine Linehan, *Sex, Secrecy, and Self-Alienation in* Strange Case of Dr Jekyll and Mr Hyde, from the Norton Critical Edition of the novel edited by Katherine Linehan (2003)

moral self-awareness".

The idea of bonds is very important in *Jekyll and Hyde*, as is the word "bond" itself. Jekyll confesses in his final document that he feels "an almost morbid sense of shame" about the attractions of pleasures he considers "undignified". He thinks it is "the curse of mankind that these undignified faggots [the 'just' and 'unjust' selves within him] were thus bound together". He tried to unbind them, he says, even before creating Hyde, by assigning them different existences, one for the day and one for the night. Letting anyone close enough to know his secret life would be unthinkable. All he can fall back on is male friendship.

Ten years before the story opens, however, Jekyll quarrels with Lanyon about the theories which lead to Hyde. This breaks "a bond of common interest" between the two men. When Hyde emerges through a process of chemical transformation, Jekyll twice describes what he feels as "a solution to the bonds of obligation".

Hyde, in other words, gives him license to act on his most reckless impulses. So when Hyde kills Sir Danvers Carew the maid who witnesses the murder says "Mr Hyde broke out of all bounds". And finally, after Jekyll has hidden himself away, he is seen immured in a "house of voluntary bondage" – destined for suicide.

If we take Stevenson at his word, then *Jekyll and Hyde* is about a man who, in Katherine Linehan's words, is the victim of a flawed assumption about human nature from beginning to end... He never credits and so never discovers sexuality's power to bridge body and soul.

Instead, he finds a way to give a "guilt-free license" to his wildest desires, becoming in the process more and more alienated from himself and "enacting through Hyde a social Darwinist nightmare of regression to the level of the child, the animal, even 'the slime of the pit'". It is a form of self-sabotage. *Jekyll and Hyde*, in this interpretation, is a vivid way of illustrating "the damage that can be done to the psyche by the sexual puritanism in Victorian society".

Oddly, if we read the novel this way it can make us feel more sympathetic to Jekyll. He is trying to live up to an unachievable level of goodness and to keep in check his reckless and unrespectable urges. Look at the way Stevenson phrases his account of the first moment of Jekyll's first chemical transformation.

I knew myself, at the first breath of this new life, to be more wicked, tenfold more wicked, sold a slave to my original evil; and the thought, in that moment, braced and delighted me like wine.

This is a vivid and surprising sentence. The second half of it seems entirely at odds with the first, and is wholly unexpected by the reader. Jekyll's wickedness, his "evil", delights him "like wine".

The consequences, though, of Jekyll's hypocricy – his two-facedness – are truly demonic. Hyde is constantly shown to us as suggestive of the devil himself. Enfield says to Utterson that "I never saw a man I so disliked". He calls him "hellish" and "like some damned Juggernaut". Utterson himself dreams of Hyde as a faceless figure and says after meeting him that he has seen "Satan's signature upon a face". Jekyll himself ends by calling him "my devil", "that child of Hell", "something not only hellish but inorganic" and "the brute that slept within".

Stevenson wrote in his essay "Lay Morals" in 1879 that the desires of flesh and spirit are likely to seem irreconcilable until a man "learn[s] to love a woman as far as he is able". Jekyll never learns to love. Instead he flees from the bonds of love and conscience. His punishment is to be haunted by a demon who dwells within "closer than a wife, closer than an eye".

How important is Victorian London?

The mood in *Jekyll and Hyde* owes much to Stevenson's atmospheric depictions of Victorian London. The city's famously dense fog continually reappears in arresting descriptions: at one moment, it is a "great chocolate-covered pall"; at another, London is "drowned" in it, so that its gas-powered lamps "glimmered like carbuncles" in a way that feels distinctly theatrical.

Seven years before writing the novel, Stevenson had written of his fondness for their "soft, atmospheric light and their "warm domestic radiance". Yet in *Jekyll and Hyde* they form the stuff of nightmares. After Enfield's anecdote about the trampling of the girl, when he describes "street after street, all lighted up as if for a procession", Utterson is haunted by visions of "the great field of lamps of a nocturnal city". He dreams restlessly of "labyrinths of lamplighted city".

These dream-images give a sense of the city going on forever. In the 19th century, London was the largest city on earth. When Enfield describes having walked home "from some place at the end of the world", his turn of phrase indicates the sheer scale of a metropolis whose population had grown from one million to six million within a century.

Nobody knew what long-term effects such a vast conurbation would have on the individuals who lived in it, but there was a profound anxiety about social unrest: as the sociologist Georg Simmel put it, the modern city gave people "a kind and amount of personal freedom which has no analogy whats-oever under any other conditions". But it could also be an oppressive place, where the individual could feel trapped, burdened by "unsatisfied yearnings"

– like Jekyll.

Stevenson's London was a place of extraordinary contrasts between grandeur and squalor. Dr Jekyll's house, with its grand front and neglected rear, epitomises the way in which these extremes were often pushed up against each other. The hall at the front of the house is deemed by Utterson to be "the pleasantest room in London". Yet viewed from the squalid rear court, the place "seems scarcely a house", rather "a sinister block of building".

The difference is so stark that Enfield, in the first chapter, doesn't even realise that it's the same place. It's as though the split characterisation of Stevenson's protagonist is directly mirrored by the architecture. Indeed, the first descriptions of the courtyard are remarkably human: the windowless upper storey is "a blind forehead of discoloured wall", the knocker-less door is "blistered and distained" like haggard, unhealthy skin.

Interestingly, it seems likely that Jekyll's house was based on a real building, one which belonged to John Hunter, a famous surgeon who had lived at No. 28 Leicester Square. The geography certainly adds up – not only was it just around the corner from Soho, where Hyde keeps his rooms, but Hunter's house also had two markedly different entrances.

At the front was a grand door on to the square itself, while at the rear a more modest entrance gave access to the now non-existent Castle Street. This entrance even had a suitably gruesome purpose: it was through the rear door that Hunter, under the cover of night, would receive the illegally procured human corpses necessary for his experiments in anatomy.

Floor plan of John Hunter's premises at No. 28 Leicester Square in 1792

How did Stevenson's own life affect the novel?

"Books are good enough in their own way, but they are a mighty bloodless substitute for life," wrote Stevenson in 1887. His short life was full of adventures. Born in Edinburgh in 1850, he travelled through Europe and later sailed to San Francisco to marry his lover, then set off to tour the South Pacific, where he died in 1894, a sickly wreck.

Edinburgh, his birthplace, exerts a strong influence on *Jekyll and Hyde*. Stevenson himself grew up in a large house in Edinburgh's "New Town" but close by, up a steep hill, was the Old Town, which fascinated young Stevenson and which he would often visit, "climbing the steep slope towards drink and debauchery", as Ian Rankin has put it. In his own bedroom was a wardrobe constructed by one William Brodie, who had been a respected citizen and carpenter by day but was a housebreaker by night. Here was "the duality of Man – not only in the figure of Brodie but also apparently built into the construction of the city itself – light and dark, the rational and the savage."

Some critics go further, suggesting that although the action is set in London's Soho, the atmosphere is really more reminiscent of Edinburgh; moreover, they argued that Stevenson was fascinated by the Scottish character, with its dual nationality (Scottish and British), and an instinctive spontaneity suppressed by the stern teachings of the Calvinistic church. "In Glasgow, where I grew up," writes the journalist James Campbell, "the common perception of Edinburgh was of a cloudy inner life (Old Town) shielded by a genteel exterior (New Town). It was – how could you avoid saying so – a *Jekyll and Hyde* sort of place."[*]

It has also been argued that Stevenson's story arose from his discreet defiance of the social pressures to adhere to Calvinist religious teaching – so Jekyll's experiment allegorically represents Stevenson's writing of the story itself.

The story is certainly strikingly different from most of Stevenson's work. For most of his life he was preoccupied with travel and exploration: one of his first books was an account of canoeing through Belgium and France, and later works like 1883's *Treasure Island* and 1886's *Kidnapped*, as well as his reports from the South Seas, all share a common theme: adventure and the unknown. In this context, *Jekyll and Hyde*, which he wrote in 1886 in Bournemouth and set in London, looks oddly out of place.

How do we explain this? To say that Stevenson himself was "a man of contradictions" might sound overly glib, but it does seem to have been the case. As the critic Roger Luckhurst has pointed out, Stevenson's contemporaries saw him

* "The beast within" by James Campbell. The Guardian, Dec 13, 2008

as an innovative literary stylist who also produced boys' adventures, pirate romances, horror stories, children's poetry, and some truly terrible plays. He was an atheist obsessed with religious questions; a workaholic who wrote "In Praise of Idlers"; a Tory who despised moralism and lived as a bohemian artist.[*]

This even goes for his adventures: suffering throughout his life with an undiagnosed heart condition, Stevenson was forced to travel in an attempt to find more amenable living conditions.

In some ways, Stevenson's eccentricities might be seen as an apt expression of his age. The global perspectives opened up by the British Empire clearly fuelled his exotic adventure stories, while the booming literary marketplace, combined with new communications technologies, meant that he could survive as a professional writer, relying on a steady income during his far-flung voyages. But only if he was willing to write things that the public wanted to read.

The clear financial impetus towards popularity made many writers uneasy. Arthur Conan Doyle, for instance, famously killed off Sherlock Holmes in 1893, preferring to devote himself to his more "serious" work – only to resurrect him later on, in return for large amounts of cash.

[*]   Roger Luckhurst, Introduction to *Strange Case of Dr Jekyll and Mr Hyde and Other Tales*

But while Stevenson and Conan Doyle have a deserved reputation for writing popular novels, both were stylish writers who explored complex ideas. Stevenson's sense of double-mindedness, for example, was evident not just in his literary work but in his attitude to politics. This "most clubbable of men", as the writer Edmund Gosse described him, was both highly traditional in his views and uneasy about the patriarchy. Similarly, he felt both pride in Britain's imperial achievements and unease about the way the empire was defended. "I was not ashamed to be a countryman of the Jingoes (i.e. an ardent patriot)," he wrote in protest against the Transvaal war in 1881. "But I am beginning to grow ashamed of those who are now fighting... We are in the wrong... blood has been shed, glory lost, and I fear honour also."

It is worth comparing Stevenson's approach in *Jekyll and Hyde* with Joseph Conrad's in, say, *Heart of Darkness* (1899) and *Lucky Jim* (1900). *Heart of Darkness* and *Lucky Jim* combine adventurous exploration with the kind of psychological introspection and dislike of imperialism that would become central to literary modernism, just as the idea of the unconscious and the primitive in man, which is at the heart of *Jekyll and Hyde* – and which caused such anxiety for the Victorians – would soon become a fertile theme in the art of the 20th century.

A SHORT CHRONOLOGY

1850 Stevenson born in Edinburgh.

1867-71 Studies engineering at Edinburgh University. Drops out to study law, then moves south to London.

1876 Meets his wife-to-be Fanny Osbourne at an artists' colony in France.

1873 Bitter dispute with his father over religion.

1880 Publication of *Deacon Brodie: A Double Life*, written with W.E. Henley. The play is not a success. Marries Fanny in San Fransisco.

1881-2 Serialisation of *Treasure Island.*

1883 *Treasure Island* published in book form, and becomes a major success.

1885 Jean-Martin Charcot demonstrates hypnotism in Paris. Stevenson moves to Bournemouth.

1886 Publication of both *Kidnapped* and *Strange Case of Dr Jekyll and Mr Hyde.*

1887 Death of Stevenson's father (with whom he

had had bitter quarrels). He leaves Britain for good, travelling first to New York, where he is already famous for *Jekyll and Hyde*.

1888 Sails to South Seas with a commission to write a travel book there.

1889 Buys a house in Upolu, Samoa.

1890 Remains in Samoa for health reasons.

1894 Dies of a cerebral haemorrhage, and buried with great ceremony in Upolu.

FURTHER READING

Jenni Calder, *Robert Louis Stevenson: A Life Study* (1980)

John G. Cawelti, *Adventure, Mystery and Romance: Formula Stories as Art and Popular Culture* (1976)

Katherine Linehan, ed., *Strange Case of Dr Jekyll and Mr Hyde*, Norton Critical Editions (2003)

Ronald R. Thomas, *Dreams of Authority* (1990)

William Veeder and Gordon Hirsch, eds., *Dr Jekyll and Mr Hyde after One Hundred Years* (1950)

BIBLIOGRAPHY

Works by Stevenson

"An Apology for Idlers" (1877) and "A Plea for Gas Lamps" (1878), in *Virginibus Puerisque and Other Essays* (Newcastle: Cambridge Scholars, 2009)

Deacon Brodie: A Double Life (written with W.E. Henley, 1880) in *Plays* (London: Heinemann, 1924)

"On Some Technical Elements of Style in Literature" (1885), in *Essays in The Art of Writing* (London: Chatto & Windus, 1905)

Strange Case of Dr Jekyll and Mr Hyde and Other Tales, ed. Luckhurst (Oxford: Oxford University Press, 2008)

The Letters of Robert Louis Stevenson, (three volumes) ed. Sidney Colvin (New York: Scribner's, 1911)

Other Works

Freud, Sigmund, *The Interpretation of Dreams* (1900), in James Strachey (trans.), *The Standard Edition of the Complete Works of Sigmund Freud*, (London: Hogarth Press, 1981)

Harman, Claire, *Robert Louis Stevenson: A Biography* (London: HarperCollins, 2005)

Hogg, James, *Confessions of a Justified Sinner* (1824), (Oxford: Oxford University Press, 2010)

Miller, Karl, *Doubles* (London: Faber, 1985)

Milton, John, *Paradise Lost* (1674), (Oxford: Oxford University Press, 2008)

Nabokov, Vladimir, "The Strange Case of Dr Jekyll and Mr Hyde", in Bowers (ed.), *Lectures on Literature*, edited by Fredson Bowers (London: Weidenfeld and Nicolson, 1980)

Simmel, Georg, "The Metropolis and Mental Life", in Frisby & Featherstone (eds.) *Simmel on Culture: Selected Writings* (London: Sage, 1997)

Truffaut, François, *A Definitive Study of Alfred Hitchcock* (New York: Simon and Schuster, 1986)

First published in 2021 by
Connell Guides
Spye Arch House
Spye Park
Lacock
Wiltshire
SN15 2PR

10 9 8 7 6 5 4 3 2 1

A CIP catalogue record for this book is available from the British Library.
ISBN 978-1-911187-15-8

Design © Nathan Burton

Assistant Editor and typeset by:
Paul Woodward

Printed in Great Britain

www.connellguides.com